Praise for

LOVE, LAUGHTER, LIFE AND THE HEREAFTER

FIFTY-NINE STORIES IN RHYME

To age with grace and wisdom, we must dodge cultural stereotypes and be on the lookout for individuals who exude an ageless aura of gusto, adventure and depth. Consider the renowned writer Simone de Beauvoir, who, late in life, wrote: "There is only one solution if old age is not to be an absurd parody of our former life, and that is to go on pursuing ends that give our existence a meaning." Or the psychologist Carl Jung who was 83 when he wrote, for his memoir: "My life is a story of the self-realization of the unconscious. Everything in the unconscious seeks outward manifestation..."

Now, echoing such insight is the work of journalist and publicist Dan Pinger who, at age 86, has written a collection of narrative poems that resound with a profound mix of levity and reality, imagination and honesty. In his own unique style, Pinger takes us to a place filled with memories, philosophies and images that may seem like the past but can also, if we listen carefully, guide us to a saner future. By adding meaning to his life through the advent of his poetry, Pinger has become a true model for engaging in a wise and mindful process of aging.

—Ann Hagedorn, author of the narrative nonfiction books *Wild Ride*, *Ransom*, *Beyond the River*, *Savage Peace* and *The Invisible Soldiers*

LOVE, LAUGHTER, LIFE AND THE HEREAFTER

FIFTY-NINE STORIES IN RHYME

By Dan Pinger

ISBN: 978-0-9980991-0-1
First Edition

Preface

The journey that resulted in this book began just several years ago, when I attempted to help my daughter who is in the Nashville music business. First, I suggested words here and there for her lyrics. Then I presented offerings in rhyme. This soon evolved to include ideas for songs. Only a miniscule portion of what I provided was used. However, a wonderful new door was opened to me.

I found that I loved digging deep into my memories, thoughts, and sometimes even creating characters and situations. I began expressing these thoughts in rhyme, at first sharing them with no one, but eventually showing a few first to relatives and then a small circle of friends. This book was encouraged.

I will be gratified if just one poem pleases one reader. Regardless, this project still is one of the greatest successes of my life. It gives my elder self new meaning. I think of these poems as beats from my heart, and hope to continue writing them as long as my own heart continues to beat.

Dan Pinger
Ripley, Ohio, August 2016

Table of Contents

The curl of an ocean wave.
Sunset blazing in far-off sky.
Miracles of the human body.
Makes one wonder why?

The world is incredible,
Beautifully organized,
Magnificently assembled,
Awesomely devised.

Yet so many young
Never had a chance,
Their lives cut short
Due to circumstance.

Wrong place, time,
Shooter guns down.
Or disease strikes,
Never again around.

Amidst world's perfection,
Why seemly mistakes?
Angry wars? Starvations?
Illnesses? Earthquakes?

Where is guiding hand?
Is all luck of the draw?
Or is our intelligence
Too limited? Too raw?

Birds kill worms.
Cats kill birds.
Dogs kill cats.
How absurd.

Why does
Life end?
Or does it,
Simply ascend?

Is death something
Not to mourn?
Because deceased
Has been reborn?

Or does all life,
While on earth,
Plant a seed
Of lasting worth?

Is true value
Of being here,
To find afterlife,
Amidst great cheer?

Or bequeathing
To this earth,
Something
Truly of worth?

Is death in this life,
Part of nature's plan,
That was conceived
Before time began?

Whichever it may be:
Afterlife? Planting seed?
All life has eternal worth.
It seems that way to me.

Omnipotent nature,
Within it a degree,
Of earthly free will.
Glorious. Heavenly.

As I am in my setting sun,
Looking back at what I've done.
What once I thought so important,
Now seems remarkably unimportant.

Everything my money bought,
That I once so desperately sought,
Is now a faded memory.
I judge it all as buffoonery.

The people I thought so unfair,
They caused me tears and to swear,
I can't even remember their names
Nor much about dispute claims.

What comes to me so clear,
So much I misjudged while here.
I should have redirected my life from the start,
Less attention to my head, much more to my heart.

Truth is what I now most treasure,
Vivid to me are my heart's pleasures.
Hugs from mom; applause from dad,
Sibling teasing, more fun I never had.

Times I kissed, and was gifted with a return,
Sweet marriages, children, stepchildren earned.
Their first steps, the things they did,
My smiles from those memories know no lid.

The smell of sweet grass, the rise of the sun,
Are my constant reminders of a good life won.
My dog at my side, cat in my lap,
Nothing will convince me there's better than that.

When my sun is totally gone,
Evening finally has arrived,
I know that these memories
Are the me that has survived.

Naked

Her summers the most joyful in life,
River village where boating is rife,
Family craft moored to the shore,
Cruising each week, perhaps even more.

Best on weekdays when few others out
She and her mother, out and about.
With packed lunch, fuel, motored from dock,
Each with her duties, worked like a clock.

One trip a lesson never to forget;
It was an embarrassment like few ever met.
When caught in life with no other way out,
Stay calm, be proud, and definitely don't pout.

Outings included a swim in waters so cool.
She would strip, jump into refreshing river pool.
Then climb back on deck, still sans swimsuit.
From ladder to deck she'd discreetly scoot.

One day came a barge, approached without a sound.
Their pleasure, her anguish, at being found.
"Stand straight and smile," encouraged her mom.
"Show you're not afraid, bravely wave an arm."

"Don't cry over milk already spilled,"
Was the lesson mother grilled.
"And when caught with no other way out,
Don't advertise the dilemma you are about."

Traditional sex education,
Tends to be only clinical.
Lacking is crucial learning,
On how to reach pinnacle.

One 10-lettered word
Leads to winning virtuosity.
Love is born and held together
Because of generosity.

Fifty percent not enough.
Give all you can away.
When both do that,
Selflessness conveyed.

Curtain opens.
Truth displayed.
Trust created.
Qualms fade.

Think not how you feel,
Focus on pleasing the other.
This then produces magic,
Known only to good lovers.

This can be difficult.
Tough work required,
To pull down shield.
When too hard wired.

Relationship mistaken,
Often for ownership.
If there signs of this,
Need to quickly nip it.

Constant communications,
Open, complete, honest,
Is an absolute requirement,
To keep romance hottest.

Never reject initial request,
To try different sex play,
Then it's for both to decide,
If new idea should stay.

The art of lovemaking.
Awkward, challenging.
Usually requires much
Practicing, managing.

He must implicitly commit
To her rhythmic pattern,
Or she rightly may fly
As far away as Saturn.

There'll be angry times,
When something cruel offends.
Satisfying sex before sleep,
By morning again best friends.

All I have learned,
In 45 years of three marriages,
Had I known them earlier:
Better wedding averages.

Matilda Takes Her Medicine 5

When I woke this morning, I felt nerves jangling in my stomach.
Today Matilda needs medicine she hates. All other thoughts
plummet.

I play it casual as I shower, brush teeth and dress.
If I indicate at all what is to come, she will be distressed.

Matilda is my German Shepherd who sees me through thick and thin,
She accompanies me everywhere; if not, knows where I've been.

She sleeps on the floor beside my bed, alert to any noise,
Running, barking, growling, any intruder she's ready to destroy.

Contrast that to when hated medicine is about to appear,
Head down, half walking, half running, for her very life she does fear.

I seldom use a choke chain, but there is no other way,
To get and control her, keep her from going astray.

In her attempts to flee, together we tumble, she and me.
She jumps in empty bathtub. Good! Cornered. Not free.

Hated pill packed in meat, carefully wrapped in pocket of my jeans,
With my hand on the leash, she knows she's out of schemes.

Place medicine in mouth, hand keeps her from spitting it out,
With eyes wide open she stares, swallows with fear and doubt.

She leaps up, runs off, by herself quietly pouting,
Then she comes. It's over. She licks. I feel like joyfully shouting.

Resilience

As I sit in my farm rocker,
Watching sun slide over ridge,
Thinking why my past pained so,
Troubles I should have bridged.

Allowed my self-worth to sink,
Cruel demons within eat away.
Heart twisted, pounded, stained,
Causing everything to turn grey.

Teenage years were dreadful.
Toted tonnage for stuttering.
Peers saw me as mocked runt.
Valueless. Sputtering. Blustering.

Girls broke our dates for other boys.
Academically, I was knucklehead.
Socially covetous, envious, angry.
Felt like I was hanging by thread.

Suddenly, one win after another.
School grades, athletics brought
Attention, parties, kissing, laughing.
Stumbling speech latent thought.

Since then so many defeats:
Wife's death, family illnesses.
Divorces. Cancers. Work setbacks.
Business closed. Money crises.

Bountiful prizes: Prodigious children,
Stepchildren, grandchildren, friends.
Exceptional employees, clients, missions,
Honors, animals, personal dividends.

Sitting, rocking, thinking, realizing,
With each trauma, anguish dwindled.
By degrees, more resilient I became.
And today, self-confidence rekindled.

Ending it all was contemplated,
At lowest point along the way.
Even considered bridge jump,
She'll be sorry she did not stay.

Now sun is about to fade,
Getting ready to turn in.
Recognize that direful sufferings,
Are among my finest wins.

Chardonnay

In my garden by the sea,
Coastal fog descends on me,
Dressed in my gown of delicate hue,
It is heaven on earth being here with you.

With our glasses held high,
Holding a wine white and dry,
We toast to the marvelous grape,
With its power to intoxicate.

Soft green plum, apple and pear,
Each complementing the other there,
It is celery crisp, vanilla and lean,
Here at this beautiful California scene.

Chardonnay, oh Chardonnay,
You certainly make hearts want to play.
You are a pure expression of wine so fine,
Each sip is a kiss; radiant, sublime.

Life is a circus,
World under one tent.
I am an aerialist,
Flying with intent.

So many opportunities,
Which ring to snatch?
Handled superb,
Or a poor catch.

Takes more than me,
To earn successful mission,
Ring has to be in reach,
To gain winning position.

Remembering childhood,
When I bloodied my sister.
Hurling bar of soap,
On forehead it hit her.

Rings. And more rings,
They keep coming my way.
Sometimes I fumble.
Others never arrive, instead stray.

In second grade,
I so much regret,
Cheating on test
A lasting upset.

My time is limited,
High on this platform.
Have to rack up wins.
I need to perform.

Took date to teen dance,
Once when in high school.
Slipped away. Never returned.
There she waited. Not cool.

Learned the hard way,
Over years of doing this.
Some wins. Many misses.
Decision making not all bliss.

I professed love to coed,
During only night of sex.
Realized truth soon after.
Refused talk. She, perplexed.

Crucial not to allow,
Blunders to slow me down,
Fretting over failed accomplishment,
Breeds lost time, more letdown.

Had a horse foundering,
Short of cash at the time,
Waited too long to call the vet.
Mare fell dead. My terrible crime.

Any bad performance from my platform
Makes me pause, ponder and pain.
Whether it be my team or just me,
Nothing short of the best is my aim.

My aging mother needed grab bar,
To steady her in and out of tub.
Leave it to me, I assured her,
Then procrastinated. Shameful flub.

Judgments of me hurt,
That is not to be denied.
Excuse team members,
Forgive. Not deride.

In leading a work team,
I try to be reasonable, calm.
Then from time to time,
My temper flares. I drop bomb.

Learned it in Sunday School,
It stuck with me ever since.
Being forgiving causes
Return of feeling like prince.

I have misjudged people,
Thought they were crooks,
Labeled them to others that way,
Only to find they live by the Book.

Much tougher when all blame,
Is locked solely inside me.
Never can flush it all away,
Too deep. Never found right key.

As I stand up here, catching rings as they come,
Aware my performance in circus nearly done.
I'm certain my history will include my transgressions.
They are part of me. Forever my scum.

Your Friends Are Always Welcome in This House 9

Jimmy veered off the highway,
Stomach upset to its limit.
Turned on a little-traveled road,
Lurched into the grass to vomit.

From his teens, he had twitching aches.
Had CAT scan, no problem found.
So he went about living his best,
Hoping health would gain ground.

He loved to hunt in the woods with dad,
Occasionally joined by older brother.
So very loved by family and friends,
Particularly girlfriends and mother.

After high school he gained entrance
Into college 100 miles away.
Twitching worsened. Grades sank.
Frustration. Daily, he'd pray.

College suggested counselor.
Long talks with him began.
Problem finally detected.
At last, they had a plan.

Dad a rough factory worker,
Shared blue jokes with the guys.
Mom was a schoolteacher,
Proper. Religious. And wise.

Must immediately come clean,
The counselor firmly advised.
Hiding is your only affliction,
Causing you to capsize.

Back in car, toward his hometown.
He drove into the night.
It is not going to be pretty.
Steadily crying. Full of fright.

"Dad. Mom. I am who I am.
I'm gay. Always have been.
Ready to face sneers.
Need my true life to begin."

Jimmy sobbed through it all.
Parents crying too.
Then dad rose, shook his hand.
As always, his words were few:

"Your friends are always
Welcome in this house."
With that, all weight lifted.
There were no more doubts.

Jimmy returned to school,
Earned two advanced degrees.
Found, married good husband.
He is at ease. Finally, free.

His mom, dad now on the road,
Campaigning for LGBT.
Imagine what their effort means
To the love of their life, Jimmy.

Entering heaven,
Was I amazed.
Standing before Mattie,
To be appraised.

Love of my life.
My best earthly buddy.
In charge of the gate.
My dog Mattie! How lovely!

She showed me
Into her study.
And explained
God's new policy.

Mattie among
Select other K-9s,
Who God considered
Magnificent finds.

All over heaven,
Most suitability.
Focus is on increasing
Animal respectability.

Mattie named Judge Superior.
Her job is to supervise
Who gets in. Who stays out.
As humans, animals at gate arrive.

She ran into our Shorty,
Love for him we share.
He was special to us on earth.
Mattie sees he gets exceptional care.

But that no-good Jack Carter.
Who regularly beat our mare,
Tried to enter. With Mattie now there,
Got nowhere. Didn't have a prayer.

If word spreads to earth,
About new pearly-gates master,
Behavior toward animals may change,
Or face heavenly disaster.

My wife's ashes,
No question,
Where they be.

Spread wide,
With affection,
With loving degree.

Childhood home,
Her suggestion,
San Francisco, by the sea.

In flowering park,
Her direction,
Under a favorite tree.

Been years since,
Joyful infection,
Sipping Chablis.

Both opinionated,
Much discussion,
Often weighty.

Serious topics,
Close connection.
Mostly agreed.

Often laughed,
Giddy elation.
Felt so free.

When with her,
Near perfection.
True jubilee.

Ashes in San Francisco,
But in clear reflection,
She's here with me.

The Love Story of Grandma and Grandpa 12

They first met in high school,
He helped with her math, she thought him cool.
She saw him often. He saw her as a jewel.
Cupid in flight, romance was adding fuel.

Soon holding hands. Going steady.
Together in all that's teen trendy.
Same college, coursework heavy.
Graduation. Good jobs. Toss confetti.

Together down the aisle. Marital bliss.
Expanded family with two kids,
On executive floor he now sits.
She's a wife and mom who never quits.

Children grow, successful in lives.
He retires, she slows, travel arrives.
Grandchildren and charity drives,
Through all, their love thrives.

Soon he confuses places. Scary!
She notices he is losing memory.
Her response: Make him feel exemplary,
As he stumbles through his reverie.

Refuse assisted living, no card games with friends.
Must keep his pride with such pretends.
In conversations, fast assistance she lends.
Always picking up any odds and ends.

Was she exhausted and stressed to the brim?
No. "It is just rewarding to be here for him.
"Never loved more," she said with confident chin.
"It's spiritual, what I do. My personal hymn."

After each day of tending, she joins him at night.
"We sleep hand in hand so he knows all is right.
When time comes for either to be taken in flight,
I know eventually we'll be joined in a new light."

Formula for Love 13

Half of all loving couples get so out of whack.
True endearment they never seem able to crack
They struggle fiercely to find the right track.,
Driven by frustration, end up on attack.

Here's the four-step formula. Follow and you'll see,
If you and your partner are suited to hold hands into eternity.
Honesty is needed. Success or failure faced. Whichever is, let it be,
Stay as lovers or leave as friends. Celebrate with glee, or politely flee.

This is a revealing but hopefully angelic love recipe.
It diagnoses the two of you, helps both to foresee,
If between you there is chemistry, empathy and ecstasy,
And in your future a ring proffered on bended knee.

All ingredients are essential. But heart is by far largest portion
Ranking a 35 percent. Any more or less may cause contortion.
Judge your true feelings by attitude and forgiveness detection.
Each should merit B plus and above for passable affection.

Now 30 percent is what your brain tells you about the person
If there's no meeting of the minds, soon may be mental coercion.
Give it thought. Do you understand the other's knotty excursions?
If only with difficulty now, as time goes by it will worsen.

Do you listen to each other, and will you in the future? That's 25 percent.
Failure to hear what the other has to say leads to torment.
Fosters discontent. Then resent. Argument. Relationship bent.
Killing something of divine worth, a loss both lament.

While only 10 percent, physical love progresses into spiritual,
But only if 90 percent is durable. Principals' worlds seem lyrical.
More sensitive, understanding, giving as never before. Not so critical.
Instead, aware of beauty, rich colors, sounds. Life's pinnacle. A miracle!

His hand touches mine,
Our fingers slowly combine.

Leaves crunch underfoot,
Rest of world seems moot.

An October chill is here,
He gently pulls me near.

A quick squeeze of his hand,
And I enter a magical land.

The faint smell of wood smoke,
Sweet, loving feelings it evokes.

Night is falling, slight breeze blows,
My tenderness for him grows.

He gestures toward a fallen tree,
Here we sit in our autumn jubilee.

I hope to be a visitor at my own funeral.
Only to see if you'd attend, act as usual.
Always so sure of yourself. Never any fears.
Wouldn't doubt if you manufactured tears.

So convincing. Smooth. You only love you.
Many words out of your mouth are untrue.
When I doubted, my thinking was rerouted.
By your charm and how sincere you sounded.

Same pattern. I was too timid to ever vent.
Borrowed from me. Repayment never sent.
It was for business in New Orleans.
It wasn't what it seemed. Come clean!

Wanted to marry; a mistake that would have been!
You took me for all, only to leave me in a spin.
My burning affection has turned to seething rejection.
Too much imperfection. Hurtful infection. Now my disconnection.

My sweet dreams came apart at the seams,
Lies by reams pushed feelings to other extreme,
However, if you attend, I would be pleased,
To watch you act as though you're bereaved.

Don't Mess with Harry

My tomcat,
Big, mighty Harry,
If human,
He'd be scary.

Tough as nails,
Brave and smart.
Don't fool with him,
He'd rip you apart.

As kitten he hid,
In deserted barn.
Freezing months,
Nearly feral, forlorn.

Loving care administered,
After being discovered,
Found can-do attitude.
Thankfully recovered.

Rose in animal hierarchy,
Now undisputed boss,
Of all my house creatures.
Harry is never crossed.

Big German Shepherd,
So full of fierce bark,
Tiptoes from Harry,
Frightened of his spark.

Routine tender meeting,
Between Harry and me,
Takes place each morning,
As I awake bed sleepily.

He's at my feet to greet,
Orange coat, eyes gazing.
Standing perfectly still,
Quietly there, just waiting.

I stroke his head again, again.
Then hold my hand down steady.
He robustly rubs his face against it.
New day. Each of us now ready.

The Art of the Obituary 17

Why are most obituaries phony?
Glowing, but all full of baloney?
Certainly the good Lord knows
How the naked truth goes?

Wife reports husband's heart quit,
Obit details his idyllic life's bliss.
Fails to mention his years spent in prison,
Habit of sleeping with other women.

Most obits seem to want to inform God,
The person sent up is worthy of His nod.
All mention of mistakes stripped from resume,
Attempting to give deceased a clean getaway.

I know love stays with a few couples forever,
But many marriages not always perfect weather.
That's the way it is. You just do your best.
God knows who's who. So don't be depressed.

Celebrity obits the exception. They report good and bad.
If you're a celebrity, warts are chronicled. A cad is a cad.
The public wants truth of those in public eye.
Won't tolerate a one-sided obit. You can't lie.

Here's my obit. I want you to get it straight.
Flunked first and ninth grade, law school not great.
Married thrice, twice divorced.
Pained my family, much remorse.

Business went bankrupt, I went broke.
Endless challenges of which I spoke.
But raised six children, so proud of that.
Created jobs for hundreds. Does that get a tip of the hat?

Helped friends in need.
Cared for dogs, cats, horses too.
Write my obit. But remember:
God knows. He's got the full view.

From Mother to Matilda 18

As a tiny child,
Everywhere I toddled.
My mother always there,
To keep me safely coddled.

Now as an old man,
Everywhere I bobble,
My dog Mattie always there,
To keep me safely throttled.

You stumble into this world
And you stumble on the way out.
Without loving mothers and dogs,
My survival would be in doubt.

Dad pushed me to win.
Failure was my sin.

He was a bigwig in town,
Hated when I let him down.

If he could say, "That's my boy."
I'd absolutely burst with joy.

Seldom happened, sorry to say.
Upon my failures his reputation weigh.

Tried hard to please him,
But everything I did turned grim.

He taught me to catch and hit.
But when choosing teams, I was last pick.

In school I flunked a lot.
Only Dad's pull kept my spot.

For failures, there was no excuse.
About them he was full of abuse.

No one could be prouder of the USA.
Greatest nation in world, Dad used to say.

Reason for this was quite simple.
Superior stock settled. Not cripple.

Winners in everything imaginable.
Quality of life here remarkable.

Only winners could create such a nation,
He said all my forefathers were sensations.

They came from England, Germany and France,
To take part in the American democratic dance.

After Dad passed, I traced my ancestry.
All were losers. Dad's majesty was fantasy.

My relatives were criminals in their homelands,
Run out by law enforcement commands.

The important lesson of this: I wish Dad had known
Importance of family history is overblown.

Pressure would have been off me growing up.
But he was my Dad. Out of respect I raise my cup.

If only he had accepted and honored who I really am.
Life would be happier instead of feeling I was not worth a damn.

I'm in love with the woman I want her to be.
Why can't she be who I want her to be?
She was Miss Right, she's becoming Miss So-So,
If things turn around, down the aisle we'll go.

She was right on time for our first date.
But ever since, she's been fashionably late.
Total disrespect for others' time,
I sit here waiting while the clocks chime.

She thinks my time should be devoted to her,
No hobby, no fishing, no pool with my brother.
Though together we have interesting fun in our leisure,
She can't understand that I might need a breather.

When she goes shopping it is a daylong journey,
Cross-examining each item as if she were an attorney.
I fret since I've already been online,
Found the best deal, bought it, saved a great deal of time.

Precise communication is just not her style,
Gross exaggeration more like it, by the pile.
If I've done something once and never before,
She says I 'always' do it. It's hard to ignore.

Take exception when she answers for both of us
Accepting invitations before we discuss.
She says she does it because she knows me so well,
But she doesn't know me at all. That's it, in a nutshell.

Too many people suffer,
Grave, personal wounds,
Excruciating. Heart numbed.
Difficult challenges to prune.

Origin may be circumstantial,
Geographical, psychological,
Psychiatric, physiological,
Or some other obstacle.

I painfully suffered tragedies,
Tried to fight through each,
Sought strong resilience.
Was Eden ever within reach?

Debilitating disorders:
My dear son, sweet mother.
Fatal cancers: dad, great wife.
Bankruptcy. Divorces. Others.

Learned language of doctors.
Rules and routines of hospitals.
Soothing talk: therapists, pastors,
Thin assurances by today's apostles.

First disaster left me empty,
Depressed, could hardly function.
Preoccupied with personal pain.
Took years to reach resumption.

When next calamity arose,
Searched deeply for real me:
"Why am I here?" "What's ahead?"
Struggled mightily to find key.

Must tackle what is possible to fix.
And focus most energy on that alone.
There may be life before birth, after death.
But presently, I rivet on here-now zone.

Decided I should participate 90 percent in life,
Reserving 10 percent to maintain spiritual within me.
When all or portion of 90 percent is taken away,
Switch to soul reserve to keep from dark sea.

I pledged to make most of the life I was given.
Focus on the present and not harbor past.
Put my all in finishing whatever mission,
When done. Switch to soul power. Recast.

This life formula might not work for everyone.
All I can say is it certainly has helped me.
I am stronger in the face of each catastrophe,
After seeking balance in reality's potpourri.

World again is laughter, gloriously berried.
My children, their spouses, grandchildren pamper.
Never imagined cosmos as wondrous as this.
Thankful, insight gained. I'm now my commander.

The Night Ripley Wore Orange and Black

Long-time enemy pulls surprising turnaround,
It was a night most thought would never arrive.
The divide between black and gold Georgetown High
And blue and white Ripley. For decades they collide.

Bad feelings began 100 years ago,
Ripley along the river, Georgetown on higher ground.
Flooding moved the county government to Georgetown.
Soreness from that decision is still around.

Basketball is popular in rural Ohio.
Most every farm has hoop nailed to shed.
Farmers' boys spend years at the sport.
This usually puts them way ahead.

Only takes five to form a team.
So no school too small to compete.
Never a shortage of wise coaches.
Dads, granddads call out to athletes.

No team in our region went so far,
As Georgetown G-Men in 2005.
Competing for state title 100 miles away.
The entire region came alive.

Cars and buses caravanned to the game.
A sea of black and gold filled the stands.
Then came another wave of G-Men colors,
Rival Ripley dressed as black and gold fans.

Tears flowed as both sides realized
What was happening then, there.
Was villages' barrier finally broken?
Are game-making differences square?

When the opponents took the floor,
Taller, athletic, faster, stronger,
Intimidating practice formations,
No doubt they surely would conquer.

Foes from an academy in big city,
Known for basketball mastery.
Slighter farm boys had no chance.
It was going to end disastrously.

Georgetown made the first basket,
Held a slim lead at halftime.
Seemed to throw to empty space.
But mate suddenly would find.

Academy boys higher, quicker, flashier.
G-Men lower, slower, calmer, smoother.
Suddenly realization hit. G-coach stood,
Allowed substitutions for each regular.

Trophy presenter fanned enthusiasm.
"Once 16, then 8, 4, 2, now only 1!
"It's G-Men now champs of the entire state."
Think of what those boys just got done:

They showed the world another way to win.
Years of learning each other's every move,
Allowed them to run circles around mightiest.
While exhibiting what vast team practice can prove.

Few were sleeping when the players' bus arrived.
Waiting crowds at high school ready to combust
Each player was introduced, a band played.
It was after midnight but the county was robust.

That included Ripley, still in gold and black,
Oh so proud of G-Men's accomplishment.
Wonder if this had happened 100 years ago?
Breaking divide. Peace-loving attainment.

Major key to success,
On this earth of ours:
Line up relationships
Which will open doors.

From birth to death,
We search for ways
To extend ourselves,
And to make headway.

A primal tactic
In achieving this:
Uncover commonality,
Get others to assist.

Diplomats practice it,
Salespersons too.
Find a common topic
With others to pursue.

An experience or wish,
Mutually shared,
Is enough to begin
Talks, thoughts aired.

Once bridge is built,
Communication widens,
Advancement negotiated,
Combined futures brighten.

I follow this practice,
When in need of a tune-up,
I sit deep in my farm's woods,
Explore how I stack up.

I look, think, feel, observe,
That we all started from seed.
Animals, plants, me, you;
On this planet we proceed.

Grow, experience,
Eventually leave.
What next depends
Upon what you believe.

Humbling to think seeding,
Is what all share in common,
The process that causes
Our universe to blossom.

When frightened of foreign,
Wondering if I have the goods,
I sit on stone boundary fence,
Hidden deep in my woods.

Trees, leaves, birds, ants, me.
Our connection: each here by seed.
When I think of it that way,
Something inside sets me free,

I flood with appreciation,
For everything I can see.
Begin to breathe deeply.
Head no longer weighty.

I've been taught the value of networking,
Meeting people to grow my business.
I've learned to use the same principle,
With nature to nurture inner fitness.

My Jacqueline

No one loves me more than Jacqueline.
Sweet as berry cream, completely without sin.

I am her man. Center of her world.
Around me, her heart unfurls.

When she looks at me with loving eyes.
The temperatures between us rise.

She understands when I had too big of a day.
And not want to enter our usual love play.

But most evenings we hug in adoring embrace,
Totally quiet. At peace with each other. Elegant grace.

This tranquil, silent passion lasts and lasts,
Until I realize it is time for our baths.

I lightly caress her face with my hands,
A tender touch she well understands.

Up we rise after another endearing evening,
Me to shower and to bed with warm feeling.

She earnestly tongue-bathes fur as far as she can reach,
Then over to her floor pillow. It has been angelic for each.

Open Heart Procedure 25

In early history,
And still true today,
In the name of God,
Upon others they prey.

Happening abroad,
As well as at home,
Attackers suffer from
Hateful syndrome.

They crusade
For their one way.
Lock their hearts,
From any other say.

An atrocious form
Of this severe disease,
Is when they kill
Those who disagree.

See this too often,
Even on our soil.
People ridiculed.
Makes my blood boil.

When children
Face zealotry.
They wonder:
"Why me?"

The immature religious,
Far from being heavenly,
Causing harm.
Acting dreadfully.

Intolerance in degrees,
With audacity to say,
Their view of deity,
Is absolutely only way.

Wider acceptance in U.S.,
Since we are a meritocracy.
A stew of religious beliefs,
Fits our representative democracy.

True issue is with the heart.
When squeezed by ignorance,
Stops flow of enlightenment.
Keeps understanding at a distance.

But when blockage is dissolved,
Causing dark shadow to lift.
Every time dissolution happens,
Derisive anger, hate drifts.

This moment not achieved by battle.
Shooting, shoving won't win.
Takes open heart and open mind,
To ring safety, happiness, peace in.

Under the Covers 26

To all married couples, this message is for you.
Never lose sight of what the two of you can do.
It is fine to be quiet, private and proper to the world
But under the covers, be free, explore unfurled.

It was eternally meant to be,
A delight for both he and she.
If that were not positively so,
Feelings would not be such a glow.

Nerve endings situated in such a way.
To produce memorable, enjoyable play.
If you can open up to one other,
Each will be an accomplished lover.

If you prefer steady routine,
Allow no other thought to intervene.
But new ways can refresh stimulation,
Increase flirtation, further elation.

Think of what spices might be appropriate,
To heighten good feelings you already create.
A touch, verse, film, look, song, book or word,
A change of pace can leave both stirred.

Living in love makes lives more rewarding;
Best when each gives all: no withholding.
Love should never be a serious matter,
Continuous fun, overflowing with laughter!

The Chase

All my long life,
Wanted way too much.
Misdirected years,
Chasing such and such.

With a desire to be seen,
At uppity gatherings,
In order to continue
Upward traveling.

King of the hill,
I wanted to be.
So an all-out push.
Constant pursuit was key.

I won. Big time.
Who's who knew me.
Whatever I said,
People would agree.

Focused on myself,
Shouldn't have let happen.
World full of too many like me,
Selfishness is a sick fashion.

As time progressed,
I eventually stumbled.
Now I realize that tumble
Made me infinitely more humble.

Lord why couldn't I
Have learned this sooner?
I could have accomplished more
As a kind-hearted mover.

My exertion now no longer
Directed on self, money, fame,
But toward family and friends,
Others' needs now my aim.

I wish I'd paid more attention,
To wives, children, others' needs,
In thoughtful, spiritual, emotional ways,
Thereby affecting more good deeds.

Love of My Life 28

Real love is there.
Has been for 11 years.
Existing between my dog and me.
Departure is near, I fear.

She moved in at eight weeks old.
We grew closer by the day.
Through her many sicknesses,
She battled disease to stay.

We understand each other fully,
Communicating with a look.
Knowing what the other wants,
To each the other, an open book.

I try to take her wherever I go.
When I can't, I explain, stroking her head:
She'll turn, flop to a favored spot,
And just stare at me. Enough said.

At night she sleeps on floor by my bed,
Protectively barking if coyotes come near.
Each morning we breakfast side by side:
Me at table, she on floor, both in good cheer.

Her health a struggle for years.
Daily takes 14 pills, most willingly,
In and out of the animal hospital,
Never gets quite fully cured seemingly.

There once were three,
Little Shorty, Mattie and me.
One day Shorty disappeared.
Found dead of old age under tree.

Between them, Mattie always led.
But if Shorty thought differently,
Shorty would stop, stand, go no further.
Mattie would return instantly.

Together they would go on journeys.
Through barns, woods, fields of farm,
Always staying within feet of one other,
To be safer, I guess, from any harm.

So I never could ascertain.
Which one *really* was the boss,
Big German Shepherd Mattie?
Or tiny terrier Shorty? I'm at loss.

When Shorty left this world,
Farm was quiet for a week.
Horses motionless. Cats hiding.
Mattie and I felt weak.

As time moved on.
We sort of did too,
Except for sensitive Mattie,
Who's still occasionally blue.

Whenever she finds,
Shorty's favorite rug,
She'll be there for hours,
Her way of giving Shorty a hug.

Both Mattie and I
Are in our twilight.
Her breed lasts until about now.
At 86, I too am near flight.

What I'll pack with me,
Are memories I own,
Of Mattie and Shorty,
Our deep attachment grown.

Rewarding lifework,
Life's major prize.
Everything else,
Not near its size.

Learned this,
After struggle,
Changing courses,
Magical juggle.

Wrong road at start,
Took nearly lifetime,
Many twists, turns,
Before my bells chimed.

Now old. So I share,
Hoping this may,
Help you decide,
Your own best way.

I lusted for power,
To face mighty seas.
When finally achieved,
Embarrassed! Wasn't me.

Went to law school,
On university's invite.
Decided against,
Lifetime of fight.

Married to three.
Lost one to death,
Two to divorces.
My sorry never left.

Favored fatherhood,
A monumental role.
Contributing to world,
Additionally, to my soul.

Daily news journalist,
Writing stories on fly.
Reported only what.
No time to dig for why.

University administrator,
Just not my cup of tea.
Academicians act slowly,
So progress never be.

Agency life fit me well.
Positive messaging,
Helping corporations.
Many happy reckonings.

Sought my fortune,
Once I had a lot.
Pained, unhappy for
Those who had not.

If I could do it over,
No mogul. It's not me.
I get my kicks from
Living a lesser degree.

Simply being a dad,
Husband, helper.
Supporting others,
Providing shelter.

Each of us is different,
Searching for our own key,
To unlock what fits best.
When heart, soul agree.

When I once found,
I knew it deep inside.
Multifaceted happiness,
Could not be denied.

Adorable couple,
Envy of all.
Both so talented,
Others in awe.

He a physician
Of wide renown,
She a society woman,
No better found.

He born in poverty,
She from rich, well bred.
When expecting first child,
Decision of doctor he led.

He assigned a mission
To his best friend,
An obstetrician
Upon whom he could depend.

Forceps delivery,
Handled too strong.
Child lived,
But mentally wrong.

Baby taken home,
With nurses 'round the clock.
Later institutionalized,
Never learned to walk, talk.

To show faith in his friend,
He had him birth the next two.
All those were successful,
But hearts of he, she askew.

No heated arguments,
Nothing like that.
Ships passing in night,
Hardly even a chitchat.

He arose early each morning
Off for hospital rounds.
Home for quick lunch, supper,
Then out. Work abounds.

She managed the children,
Attended to their many wishes.
Enjoyed Ladies Bridge Club
Active in church. Cooked fancy dishes.

While maintaining their high esteem,
For all the world around them.
The painful loss must have done it.
Twisted their hearts numb.

Whether the true cause was too personal,
(For he, up from poor, and she, so privileged,)
To admit and seek professional help.
Kids too hurt. Forever emotionally damaged.

He, she led full lives and died,
Widely heralded as great people.
If only they had dug deeper,
And not left with hearts so feeble.

Was it the forceps alone?
Putting faith in a friend again?
Differences of their backgrounds
Causing difficulty, strain?

Or was it pride not admitting failure?
Marriage without shared laughter?
Blind to needs of spouse? Only self?
Pray each finds love, peace in hereafter.

Decline of a Rural News Outlet

31

News nerve center,
In my rural town:
Is where stuff's decided,
Who's up; who's down.

Judgments made,
Six mornings a week.
Coffee. Toast. Talk.
Men retirees' clique.

Always at corner table,
In village Burger King.
Was eight. Now seven.
Death took one in Spring.

Each has network,
Of family, friends,
Gathering gossip,
For purposeful ends.

Stories are shared,
Commented upon,
Set for distribution,
For all to dwell upon.

News comes in, goes out,
Again by families, friends,
Packaged at Burger King,
As far as interest extends.

This community asset,
Existed for generations,
Old die. New join.
Panel has fluctuations.

But now it's weakening,
Interest in product slipping.
By time messages leave table,
News of the day already nipping.

Social media has blown hole,
In time-old community service.
Much of news no longer new,
Much of function worthless.

So now past dwelled upon.
Memories still fairly clear.
What happened in '38,
They'll either cheer or jeer.

Comparing back then to now,
An often heated discussion.
Strong opinions expressed,
Of topics' repercussions.

For example, they concluded,
Yesterday after 90 minutes,
Modern toothpaste tubes,
Have intrinsic inherent limits.

In old days, tubes had keys,
To twist all paste from vessel.
Today some paste left behind.
No matter how hard you wrestle.

Another day, another topic,
Or maybe not. They gather,
For what they believe serious.
Often amounts to blather.

Whole town knows where they are,
From six to eight they still go at it.
Hoping they find enough to talk about,
Now that breaking news no longer fits.

Added to decline of importance,
Youngsters know everything first.
They text what happened to whom,
Senior self-esteem now reversed.

Some questioning continuation,
After current members fall.
Popular opinion: it will function,
Since oldsters enjoy memory recall.

In (app) Judgment

32

I dreamed, I searched,
Opened programs to find,
Good, bad in all persons,
Only platform of its kind.

With iPhone photo, birth year,
Degree of goodness determined,
Scope ranging from saint to Nazi,
From lovable to worst vermin.

Software instructions explain:
There is no 100 percent either way.
No human is absolutely fine,
Nor one utterly decayed.

When I was a journalist,
Interviewing clerics to crooks,
Ohio prison warden told me,
It's not always how it looks.

Inmates with worst offense,
Often really are true gentlemen.
Slipped just one hour, one day.
Spend rest of life in this pen.

Grain of bad in everyone,
As well as pinch of good.
Quantity of which kind,
Needs to be understood.

Dilemma forever:
Determining ratio.
Love lost, hate,
For lack of know.

I was stunned,
After first use.
Love is what,
Eighty percent produced.

Seemed high.
But even so,
Much past 50 percent,
Surprising show.

Bad's measure:
In low 20s.
Placing worth:
Only pennies.

Carry program,
On my app,
Truth there,
To be cracked.

My life changed,
With this tool.
Snap judgments,
Only for fools.

Tornado Alley

33

I'm in painful tornado alley of lovers.
Hot, heart spinning, face turning colors.
Moments ago, love was peaceful and tender.
Now I feel I'm in a violent storm's center.

Packing an incredibly vicious vocabulary,
Machine-gunning words. They are her cavalry,
Leaving a path of destruction that's scary.
Puzzled why she thinks of me as adversary.

After the tempest, calm settles in,
No trace of battle there had been.
We sail smooth waters for weeks,
Long talks. This must be for keeps.

Months later I expressed helpful hint.
To improve lifestyle by just a glint.
She resisted. Unsure she understood.
Explained; felt like talking to wood.

Frustrated. I screamed. She's sobbing.
All over my bit of advice. Shocking.
Took hour for squall to subside.
What to do when feelings collide?

Now married, when gap unsolvable,
Invoke our vow to make it resolvable.
While both in no mood to follow through.
We together turn with no hullabaloo.

Force ourselves to physically be close with other.
Cuddle. Kiss. Make love. Peace recovered.
It's way out after pinned in tornado alley.
Next morning skies clear. From strife to rally.

Charlotte

34

Charlotte, gorgeous in every way.
Face, body like well-formed clay.
Eyes from which you can't turn away,
Hair knowing its position to play.

Sass, causing men to think risqué.
Mind a steel trap. Always straight As.
Dress fitting for any place, any day.
Attention-stealing date at any cabaret.

Believe me, guys, beware,
Trouble if you go there.
Never will you ever snare,
Only to leave in despair.

First date always bliss,
But never even tiny kiss.
Second date amiss, strange one, this.
Third, final loud hiss.

It's the way she's been for years,
She's aware. Caused her tears.
I have known her all my life,
Always this third-date strife.

She seems up for changes,
Appears to need new ranges.
Always immediately halts,
Claiming newfound faults.

She likes total freedom,
Of her own kingdom?
She is exceptionally dynamic,
Just moments later frantic.

Yes, she is unconventional.
So gifted, multi-dimensional
She could be such a winner,
Instead, wrung in ringer.

Holding Course

35

Puffs of wind
To fill my sails.
Needed if
To prevail.

Can't be weak.
If to succeed,
Must meet goals,
To achieve.

But not too strong,
Or I may fail,
Overshooting mark,
Success derailed.

Important lesson,
Must remember,
Perfect alignment,
Brings sailing splendor.

Compass. Experience.
Charts of the sea,
Gets me directed
To where I want to be.

Now underway,
With wind at my back,
Destination in view,
Then suddenly, whack!

Voyage failing,
Aimlessly drifting.
No firm rudder,
Direction is shifting.

Is it too much
For me to master?
Getting all together,
To avert disaster?

Power forward. Verify.
Then hold course.
Must do it all
To assure no remorse.

Never reach ideal.
But I keep trying.
Hope to get closer,
By continual applying.

With Apologies to John Lennon

36

What if early childhood experts
Instituted a curriculum worldwide,
To universally change the behavior
Of all children when applied?

Aim would be to wipe out
All competitiveness with others,
Redirecting misspent energy,
Toward own inner-self wonders.

Graduates of this training
Would never want to war.
There no longer would be sides,
Fighting would become a bore.

Relationships wouldn't suffer jealousies.
Whenever something seems to need fixing,
Focus would be on introspection. Find problem.
Root it out. Keep the rot from mixing.

All sports would be,
Of various self exercises.
Fun in pushing one's self,
To be better than one realizes.

Politics would not be tricky.
Positions, platforms expressed.
Public clear. Makes choices,
Politicians not beating their chests.

Think of all gamesmanship gone.
People interacting truly with respect,
Working within their chosen skill set.
And those flagrant falsehoods wrecked.

Individuals no longer distracted,
By all the shoving for position.
Sincere cooperativeness,
Becomes everyday condition.

World filling with professionals,
Doctors, writers, financiers too.
Programmers, teachers, farmers,
All doing what they love to do.

Is all this a dream? Yes, of course.
Not going to happen anytime soon.
But while dreaming of a better world,
Why not shoot for the moon?

A Delicate Balance

37

Nothing more challenging,
To me on this earth,
Than to find delicate balance,
In making decisions of worth.

To properly sift hard issues,
For discovery of proper mean,
Judging competing evidence,
Then usually deciding in between.

My quandary based in many areas.
Family. Business. Health. Home.
Religion. Readings. Writing choices.
Entertainment. I roam and comb.

Lincoln wrote perfection for Gettysburg.
An address that pulled together extremes.
Streisand hits purest notes in song,
Laser aligned to music's beams.

Queen Mum calmed war-torn England,
Silently visible amidst fiery destruction.
Lou Gehrig taught appreciation for life,
In his farewell near-death reflection.

All those required choices:
Conscious, unconscious stands,
Circumstances. Various sources.
Quibbles. Studies and strands.

Dennie, most remarkable friend and colleague,
Heard my work deliberations most every weekday.
Weighed with me this and that, we found symmetry.
Helped to pierce my fog. Showed me the way.

So easy to swing far left or far right.
At times extremes may have value.
My tendency is to move out toward sides,
Mostly then realizing it's wrong avenue.

Knowing my weakness, I strive
To broaden my selections,
Trying to hone my thinking skills,
To make conclusive connections.

Try to see all sides,
Of issues I am facing,
Hunt for equilibrium,
Truth is what I'm chasing.

Medicine Woman's Daughter 38

Horrors felt in the Great Depression,
Young Minnesota families no exception.

Polk County's harsh winters tough on rural poor,
No work. No money. Life nearly impossible to endure.

Mindy's husband traveled far for only work he knew,
To lumber camp in North where vast forests grew.

Both newly immigrated. Didn't speak the language,
Understood only Norwegian, a competitive disadvantage.

They had a child, Betty, who this story is about,
Achieved much after having nothing starting out.

No running water. No inside toilets. No electricity.
Only a potbelly stove needing wood fed it regularly.

Husband gone, Betty just 3, Mindy searched to survive.
Made moonshine to sell to keep her and Betty alive.

Soon throughout the county her product in great demand,
Fourth-hand car for deliveries over twisting roads of land.

One black night it happened. She drove into a trap set by the law.
A deadly crash. Betty now homeless; her dad she never again saw.

Cousins stepped forward, no one to take full responsibility,
So Betty was passed from one to another, a show of civility.

At 14 she went to live alone in an apartment in town,
Sought schooling because intellect in her did abound.

Junior college, then college scholarships, a move downstate to teach.
Married. Four children. All-American dream is in reach.

Together, they built a home. Furnished it nicely. Got a new car.
Memorable family vacations. As parents, superstars.

Husband held three jobs. She studied for Master's degree.
All children college educated; from poverty they are free.

Given the upbringing, Betty as resilient as anyone on this earth.
She raised herself. She built a better life, for all it is worth.

A Bit Less Outer

I have appeared to be up,
While really feeling down.
Other times through frown,
Was quietly relishing renown.

Root of problem, I believe,
Part of me gregarious,
Other piece reclusive.
So sometimes stiffness.

When in business,
The world was loud and fast.
Need for solitude.
Retreat. Walk. Recast.

I often had to push,
To shake hands and greet,
While in my inner self,
I was feeling incomplete.

In Myers-Briggs blend,
Measuring outer, inner,
I've tested a bit less outer.
It is as is. All are winners.

My personality near pivot,
Easy to slide either way.
In mid-conversation,
May have no more say.

Enjoy sharing silence,
With those of like nature.
Then my burst of gab
Considered odd behavior.

Likewise, in chitchat,
I've suffered losses,
When I ceased interest,
Inward to other focuses.

Horrible in first marriage,
Wife pondered my flights,
I'd been in her reality,
Then abruptly off like a kite.

Mistakenly thought footing firm,
She silently plotted divorce.
After night of food, love and fun,
She left with little remorse.

Different with next wife.
Tried harder. Each comfortable.
Gave each other plenty of space,
Conduct never combustible.

Lesson I learned from this:
In prized relationships,
Likely she and me,
Not on identical scripts.

I first knew her when we were both four,
She was one to play tag with, nothing more.

In second grade I think she was in my class,
Never noticed, maybe, I think she was, alas.

By fourth grade she could throw a football, make it spiral,
Play the game as good as any guy, no denial.

In sixth grade she didn't run or shout any more,
Disappeared on walks with girls, us she would ignore.

Seventh and eighth grades strange and full of mystery,
Her talk and actions friendly, then suddenly turn blistery.

In the ninth, we boys partied with soda and chips,
Then made visits to where she was with other chicks.

Can't remember one thing ever said at those meetings,
Teasing, giggling, smiling, happy feelings.

Next summer, she invited me swimming at town pool,
That fall on afternoons, I'd walk her home from school.

Regular dates each Friday, watching TV with friends,
Saturday was special, with others or not, all depends.

The beginning of junior year, decided we were ready.
Announced to family and friends that we were going steady.

Bought an old car with savings from after-school jobs,
So I could drive more places, see more of my heartthrob.

Upon graduation, got a job and joined the National Guard,
With both incomes, providing for her would not be hard.

I proposed on one knee, she agreed, planning for a big wedding,
Then unexpectedly got the call, to war I was heading.

Was only a year until I would return, giving us time
To plan wedding details, where we'd live our life sublime.

I was with my buddy when he died, explosion got him,
We had just exchanged places. Such fate. Brain bursting at the brim.

"Take this," I was handed pills by some guys at the base,
They said all that bad junk in my head it will chase.

The year's tour up, back home by now, but no longer myself.
Out of control. I steal for pills to clear the junk itself.

Our wedding was tiny because of my shame.
She insists she loves me. Claims I'm not to blame.

When pain hits my heart, I go astray.
With her by my side, I pray to find my way.

Did I Mention That I'm 86? 41

I love milking my age.
It's a hilarious advantage.
For being over 80,
Allows me to be outlandish.

I sing in church at top of lungs.
Don't care what others think.
It's giving myself a reward,
After years of staying in sync.

When I can't understand talk,
No longer hearing each word,
I change the topic from sane,
Abruptly advance to the absurd.

A favorite told in ultra-polite gatherings,
About famous stripper Rose La Rose.
She chose me from the audience,
To help her off with most of her clothes.

I often ask callers to repeat over 'n over.
It's usually a business seeking information.
I tell 'em of phones covering both mouth, ear,
In old days we wouldn't have this frustration.

It's all a struggle to still be relevant,
While my hearing, walking ability fleeting.
My gross unconventional behavior,
Wants to believe decline I'm beating.

Love Story

Pay attention, dear one, never forget,
You are the most genuine of all I've met.

Overflowing with heart, sweet soul begets,
Moving forward in life, onward without regret.

For you I treasure a new kind of love,
Not one that fits in the usual glove.

But instead guided by heaven above,
Transcending all others, a high-flying dove.

We've yet to share religions, politics, no matter.
Every time I am with you makes my heart clatter.

After seeing you, good memories are fatter.
I feel like dancing, black tux, cane, high hatter.

It is magic, but would firmly turn my back,
If I knew it best for you to follow a different track.

Your welfare, happiness means more, best I pack,
Life is full of twists, turns, a tough nut to crack.

With that caveat in mind, you definitely need to know:
I love you. It is real. I love you. It is so.

I want church to help me get into Heaven.
Need to join before the angels beckon.
Decided today at friend's funeral session.
Pray overlooked will be my transgressions.

Catholic, Protestant, Muslim, Jewish,
Which denomination should I wish?
Want to pass into land of bliss. How?
For answers, I need to fish.

Selection limited to my neighborhood,
Convenience for friends would be good.
Then to the Internet. Learn what I could.
Read, then review, until all is understood.

Each has its own revered allure.
Golden Rule central to all for sure.
Spiritual rewards in each endure,
Carefully select for Heavenly cure.

Since most churches nearly equal,
Need one where friends are visible.
Membership rules must be livable.
Choir music masterful, irresistible.

When day comes, service mostly music.
Choir, soloists perform spirituals, classics.
Message of euphony must be lucid.
For funeral service to be galvanic.

Housekeeping

The quantity of dust bothers me little.
But makes uptight friends cringe, belittle.
I can live fine with it. To me, it's unseen,
While others say it is filthy, obscene.

I can't understand why they complain.
It just lies there, doesn't attack, nor cause pain.
All the energy spent being pristine,
Means missed pursuits, a less productive scene.

Less time on cleanliness, more solving problems,
Instead, concentrate on ridding mind's toxins.
More time for loved ones, for outings, for sports,
Make lasting memories, good times of all sorts.

Happy not to be a cleaning machine,
Instead, I stick to a better routine:
Dust once a year. Sweep, mop too.
If anyone differs, I tell them to shoo.

Rate fates at Heaven's Pearly Gate.
Whose chances of entry great?
Only angels can truly evaluate,
Determination of future state.

Mr. Johns gave millions to arts,
Thereby brightening many hearts.
Across nation's many parts.
Funded struggling artistic starts.

Made wealth using controls,
Profited by low payrolls,
His employees feel like moles.
Turnover constant barrel rolls.

Greg in school was a scholar,
Then divorced. Couldn't make a dollar.
Living under bridge in squalor,
Dog his only faithful follower.

His head spins from Jim Beam.
Drugs, they make him feel supreme.
But when dog falls sick, to vet to be seen.
That dog is in his every dream.

Rev. Henry, popular pastor.
High morals broadcaster.
Rating climbing ever faster,
Then came utter disaster.

After many of his seeds sown,
In church, women living alone.
Horrified as shame is known.
So he runs away into unknown.

What is your view?
Who gets through?
In each good chew,
There is truth to undo.

Pity those upstairs sorting it out.
With super information clout,
Can they see what it's all about?
Or perhaps they still all have doubt.

If I walked into party blindfolded,
I would know if you are there.
A message inside me unfolded,
By some sense extremely rare.

I know not where this comes from,
Is there some cosmic connection to you?
When you're near, my chest drums,
Feeling more alive than I ever knew.

When you leave for any length of time,
I see, hear you in everything I do,
Your lips of honey, your heels that chime,
You are warmth that continues to accrue.

The Great Creator was exceptionally artful,
Heart, personality, every way of judging,
Made you with light-up-the-world sparkle,
You are a person I can never stop loving.

At tony uptown NYC café,
In conversation with Millie.
She questioned the worth of talk:
Said 10 percent meaty; the rest silly.

Only value in empty chatter,
Said Millie, sipping coffee drink,
Is when used to open dialogue,
Grasping toward meaningful link.

Revalorization when that happens,
Chitchat now turns purposeful,
Millie guesses this exists 40 percent,
Leaving 50 percent prattle, farcical, terminal.

My number worse. Fear it's 70 percent.
So I pledge to stretch mind, heart,
Push 100 percent, prospect for verbal gold.
Bet Millie would call that being smart.

It'll gain more in conversational listening,
Carefully connecting, accepting or rejecting.
But I need time to perform those functions,
To shape a response worthy of conversing.

When fail to pull thoughts, words together,
While conversational partner waiting.
Any hope of good discussion fades.
Then it's tittle-tattle. How frustrating!

Need to persevere: Hear more, speak more,
For broader knowledge of everything.
It is lesson learned from Millie,
One to which I will cling.

State of Mind

Is your love life full of ache and pain?
Are you as happy as you should be?
The problem may be with your brain.
Not your heart washing you to sea.

People grow in different directions.
Two once close can grow apart.
Takes thought to reconnect affections.
For love again to flow from heart.

Love is a state of mind.
Mind trumps heart most time.
Use mind when need of climb,
To return love life to its prime.

Think what state of mind can do,
Helped to bring two together.
When both grow to different views.
Thought can brave love-storm weather.

Requires searching, facing differences,
Learning if each is willing to compromise.
Acknowledging ignorance, distances.
Deciding degrees willing to sacrifice.

Mental world is there to conquer,
Wise persons found after study
Mind is there to use and ponder,
Roads less muddy, lovely.

Everyone's world sometimes crumbles,
For some, there are many such tumbles.

Death, sickness, poverty, injury,
Job failure, all lead to much misery.

No doubt love loss is a leading cause,
When your adored presents you with a list of flaws.

I've endured deathbed sickness, foreclosure,
Both certainly enough to lose my composure.

But what tore me apart were two divorces,
They struck me numb with Titanic forces.

If any of these horrors ever happen to you,
Take this from one who has seen them through.

Take a deep breath. Don't rush your head.
One thought at a time, steadily move ahead.

Know you are an important person on this earth,
Focus on what's before you. Give it all your worth.

Meet new people. Be open about your problem when asked,
But don't dwell. Learn about them and positives of their past.

Eat well. Sleep well. If you are improving, become frisky?
You made it through. Toast yourself with great whiskey.

Love? Please tell me:
What about it is so?
Married three. At 86,
Still, I don't know.

Systemically organized it's not,
No scientific knowledge.
No real explanation for
Its glowing wattage.

Genuine affection,
Sweet tenderness,
Seemingly appears,
From the wilderness.

It has cuddled us since birth,
In so many degrees and ways.
Grabbing, warming our hearts.
Ostensibly with unseen rays.

This unexplainable force,
Seen in parental nurturing.
Friends and mentors guide us.
Dearest sweethearts caring.

Those who give help,
Gain from investment.
Inside their hearts,
Satisfying refreshment.

It is magical when,
Of two lovers shine,
Affecting all around,
Making stars align.

If devotion levels differ,
Causing awkwardness and pain,
Try fix? Or move on? Don't let drip?
Too wide a gap just not sane.

Love initiators have courage,
In designing, taking leap,
Hoping for relationship deep.
Failures bring tears. Weep.

True-love breakup impossible,
Fraction always stays,
There to be called upon.
Memories of bygone days.

That's all I know.
Help me if you can.
Been searching for years,
Still don't understand.

It has cuddled most of us since birth,
In so many degrees and ways.
Filling our hearts, boosting us up.
Leaving us ablaze and dazed.

Love! A God-given force:
Mom nurturing, family rearing,
Mentors fostering, friends caring,
Work promoting, many cheering.

All who invest their love,
Gain from investment.
Could take time,
To realize assessment.

Beneficiaries in its golden glow,
Ones once lost. Now they see.
Powerfully become sympathetic.
Gain in heavy doses of empathy.

Its origin? Lord only knows.
It seems to be an organism,
That divides. Flying pieces alighting.
Delighting. Causing heart spasms.

Beats often not same intensity.
Hesitations by one while other shines.
It is Utopia when both chip in,
Making stars in heaven align.

Love initiator benefits most,
For designing, taking leap.
Hoping for relationship deep,
Yet failures bring tears, weep.

When that happens, some is lost.
But a fraction always stays.
Always there to be called upon,
As a warm memory of bygone days.

You're better person having tried,
Adding to your life's accumulation,
Of all love-particle references,
In your inner carrier of information.

This will be you until you pass.
When your particles join others.
Your collection you brought is hailed.
It is what you are, like none other.

Too Many Hobbled Toads on Road of Life

Heaven above doesn't want you stuck,
For decisions once great, now amuck;
Bonds once chosen to guide your way,
May no long be for you in your new day.

When your head and heart begin to say "enough,"
And past meets present, do you bluff or rebuff?
Reevaluating your inner spirit regularly is a must,
If you are going to keep your soul without rust.

Too many today fail to take the painful road,
Ending up trudging through life as a hobbled toad.
Hanging onto to the past which now has turned grim,
Personal potential drained. It is beyond sad. It's a sin.

Others conclude their choices have been correct,
Now feeling better that they had them checked.
So continue in their position with energy renewed,
Having examined, learned; head and heart no longer skewed.

Unfortunately, it's not so easy in this age of change,
To stay in one place in a world that has turned strange
Divorces skyrocketing; job turnover reeling; people relocating.
Need to stop to learn what your inner self is now resonating.

Those who fight change, refuse self-examination, are a sorry lot.
They trudge like that wounded toad until they are gone and forgot.
The winners are those who face change all around them and within,
And honestly judge the wisdom of their contemplated new begin.

It is interesting to note from my first-hand knowledge,
I fought many battles to stay the course, I acknowledge.
After all the heartache of loss, pain and change I suffered,
Each time, each one involved saw greater happiness uncovered.

Richer or Poorer

53

Takes no money to feel rich,
Even when you don't have a stitch.
To someone who has not,
Little things can mean a lot.

Billionaires can think they're poor,
While living amidst all their grandeur.
Many are in constant fear,
That all their wealth will disappear.

If you had to pick, would you want to be
Poor or rich? What would you decree?
I take being poor any day,
Enjoying the free wonders of life's buffet.

Many rich have too much pain and worry,
Making them agitated, bustling, blurry.
While the poor can lead a life of discovery,
Local miracles. An interesting luxury!

Straight Talk

Some are so difficult to understand.
Can't just tell you stuff man to man.
Making a point in such roundabout way,
Lengthy road using problem word displays.

I asked a girl to a movie,
She said something about Tuesday,
Her mom, a pet fish, a Jacuzzi,
Paris. Left Bank. All made me woozy.

Just as bad was college football player,
My roommate, a quarterback slayer.
His vocabulary you can count on your toes.
Sentences incomplete, listener woes.

When I sought permission from my lawyer-mom to play,
She judged it as a legal case with many factors to weigh
Exploring safety, playmates' character. Is cloud too gray?
By time her answer came, my friends had gone on their way.

Our preacher talked, each word in a deep baritone distinctly,
Seemed disconnected beyond earth, coming across creepy.
Holy he was not. Congregation voted to seek his resignation,
After pastor was jailed several times for booze preoccupation.

Who am I to talk about good sense in verbal communications?
Born a stutterer, spent 25 years with its painful frustrations.
Began a sentence, I never knew if I could get across the thought,
People waiting. Not knowing which way to turn. My attempt to speak
for naught.

This is the way it usually goes:
I ask my heart, the one who knows.
Am I in love? Is that what flows?
I feel its possibility, I suppose,
Adoration for each other glows.

Suddenly some compatibility woes,
Love not 100 percent now shows,
Before, we just weren't on our toes,
Relationship now is in throes,
Questions about togetherness grows.
Decide to walk before we come to blows.

Been through it often. Time and again,
Discovering incongruity every now and then.
Soon it begins to painfully offend.
Magic fades. Continue? Should we pretend?
Best to part friends. Call it an end. Amen.

When life is full of storms,
Need not be forlorn,
It takes rain to grow,
Develop into beautiful rainbow.

She announces she's through,
Found someone better than you,
Never know who next you might meet,
Perhaps someone more lovely and sweet.

Lose your paycheck after so many years,
How to manage creates deep fears.
An Internet posting could lead your way,
To a financially rewarding job offer array.

Illness overtakes your child,
Doctors puzzled, you and wife wild.
Specialist is consulted at medical center,
Could cause sickness to surrender.

Reservations made, trip paid in advance.
Storms hit. Beach, hiking no longer can chance.
Make new acquaintances, talk, play card games,
They become treasured friends, lifelong gains.

Promotion for you given to another,
When his qualifications next to yours smother.
Keep your head down. Continue at good pace.
You'll move ahead of him in the race.

I found rare opportunities,
As obituary writer,
Learning lives of the departed,
Made me feel wiser.

Found their relatives, friends, colleagues,
Probed whomever knew deceased well,
About successes, failures, flaws
Discover true life to tell.

From corporate heads to homeless,
Chosen for notoriety, narrative quality.
Some led lives refreshingly novel,
Others from distinguished ancestry.

Posthumous fame bestowed.
Upon unlikely heroes,
For having worked quietly,
Accomplishment sans egos.

Obits can get falsely sweetened.
Only to ease pain of family catastrophe.
Anguish resolution should take other forms.
Dishonesty never truly corrects history.

Each day I would come to work,
A remarkable subject waiting,
To walk me through a life well lived.
Fascinating, and worth celebrating.

They became my friends,
Though we never really met.
They became role models.
I followed paths some set.

My obit reporting ended years ago.
Now I'm old, just glad to be alive.
Wondering how my own obit will read,
Would I be pleased, surprised?

Faults here, there and everywhere
Caused me troubles by the lot.
Mixed with what I thankfully conquered,
In my obit it all needs to be caught.

He had been a scholar,
MIT Engineering degree.
She had intellectual stars
In her family's stellar tree.

He was quick, fun, interesting,
A pure joy to be around.
Her humor lighting fast.
Such hilarity would astound.

Wars cause causalities.
Many remain out of sight.
Inflicting other tragedies.
Developing after the fight.

Both constant seekers of knowledge,
Reading two to four books a week.
Loved to tiptoe into woods, fields.
For rare birds they would seek.

They threw themselves into life,
Mostly successful in every role.
Bird watcher not warrior,
He being of sensitive soul.

He had dropped hundreds of bombs,
Flying in European Theater of War.
Nazi Germany must be stopped,
Have to find way to better score.

Using our nation's best of best,
Raids were strategically carried out.
But missions failing. U.S depressed,
With its airplane, weaponry clout.

Raids constant. Planes darkened skies.
So much effort with few yields,
Bombs seldom hit intended targets,
Instead: villages, families, farm fields.

He invented many changes.
Created a new bomb-sight design.
Was decorated as a national hero
As the bombs hit targets fine.

This caused the enemy to rethink.
White flag soon began flying.
He went home. Hero in demand.
But kept thinking of all the dying.

He played a role in so much death.
His heart fixed on all the humanity,
Restlessness set in. Demons descended.
He, she met, seemingly curing his agony.

It was love at first sight, a torrid affair.
Both full of joy, having much in common.
Deeply in love. They were married.
Produced two daughters. Awesome!

After a while, torments returned.
He reading morning, noon and night.
Constant smoking, heavy drinking
Engrossed in novels as long as head held upright.

Fell asleep with book in hand,
Lit cigarette dropping from lips.
While wife, children slept
Small fires due to these slips.

His death was from heart failure.
It was sudden. Only in his 40s.
She left alone to provide for daughters
Life forward would be a squeeze.

She now needed to father and mother.
Decisions made with single goal in mind.
Her girls come first before anything else.
No way will they ever be behind.

All his Social Security money went
For girls' education, recreation.
Total of family living was fueled,
By her hard-work compensation.

So the girls had music lessons, gymnastics,
Church, soccer, trips to historic places.
Museums, theatre, educational vacations.
Yard landscaped into playground oasis.

Both girls grew to be happy, successful,
They would make any parent mighty proud.
She fought for this with every inch of herself,
To raise them to directly face the world unbowed.

True, their father was a genuine war hero,
Then became its tortured casualty.
Their mother certainly a hero too,
For way she grappled after-victory calumny.

Praise Be It to the Valley of Silicon

59

Look to the Heavens,
Say thankful prayer.
World peace is near.
Humanity heading there.

Every village fights crime,
Selfish committing offenses.
So world will need to maintain,
Force to keep adequate defenses.

Past wars tools of fools,
People didn't have say.
Drowned in propaganda,
Kept understanding away.

Were those fools unwise?
Was their logic light?
Either way, wars fought,
With no profound insight.

Definition of word "foreign"
Is changing to mean,
More than spatial distance.
Worldwide communication seen.

With Twitter, Instagram, Skype, iPhone,
These learning instruments around world.
People in real time hear, see what's going on.
First-hand knowledge is their sword.

They connect, converse, befriend,
Get to know other's cultures.
Comfort-levels broaden. Respect expands.
Far-distant populations no longer vultures.

So much chatting over fences,
Collapsing prejudices.
Toppling ignorance.
Deflating pessimists.

World to become one big village,
Legal systems universally fair.
Languages generally understandable.
Education quality climbing everywhere.

With high-caliber workforce,
Economy thriving around globe.
Massive military expense no longer.
Money for health, welfare, hope.

True enlightenment coming.
World one village undivided.
Happy, safe, knowledgeable,
Because Silicon Valley provided.

Poems by Theme

Stories About Love

Stories About Laughter

Stories About Life

Stories About the Hereafter

About the Author

Dan Pinger has played many roles in his long and eventful life. He raises horses. He served in the U.S. Army. He was a notably indifferent law school student. As a newspaper reporter, he covered the wild and woolly days when the Mob ran Newport, Kentucky. He also spent some time in academia, working as an administrator at the University of Cincinnati. But it wasn't until he turned 50 that he discovered his true calling, when he founded the Dan Pinger Public Relations agency. Dan and the hundreds of "Pingerites" who worked with him offered communications counsel to clients across Cincinnati and the nation for more than 25 years. He always said those were the most emotionally rewarding years of his career.

And of course, Dan is a father, a son, a husband, living through all the joy and heartbreak those roles bring.

Now in his 80s, Dan has begun scribbling some poems. As the title makes clear, these "stories in rhyme" deal with love (spiritual and carnal), personal and business tribulations, and an 86-year-old man's consideration of what comes next. Oh yes: And pets. Dan loves animals, and this collection includes several tributes to his favorites.

Some of these stories are true. Some of them are nearly true. Some of them are works of imagination, but grounded so much in the real world that they seem like they must be true. All of them are fiercely and unflinchingly honest.

Acknowledgements

This project would have never landed safely without Bob Kraft, editor, and Ellen DePodesta, publisher.

Bob is a retired managing editor of a major metropolitan daily newspaper, famous in journalistic circles for writing attention-getting front page banner headlines seconds before deadlines as well as guiding his staff in finding news and seeing to it that it is well written. Many of the poem titles in this book are from his clever mind.

Ellen is a Chicago marketing professional and a former vice president of my Cincinnati public relations firm. She, with her going-a-mile-a-minute mind, has pulled together all that it takes to publish this book, from overseeing cover design to the assembly of the stories on the printed pages. The poem in this book entitled Marian is a memory of Ellen's mother and my beloved wife.

I would also like to thank all of those friends, loved ones and acquaintances who have helped shape my life and the stories on these pages.

Made in the USA
Middletown, DE
27 October 2016